FAST BIBLE SUMMARIES

By Pure Truth Publications

Genesis through Deuteronomy
Joshua through 2 Samuel
Davie through Malachi minor prophets
Jeremiah through Ezekiel
I kings through Esther
Proverbs through Isiah

FAST BIBLE FACTS

- **6 Billion.** More than 6 billion copies are estimated to have been published[1] The Bible is the best selling and most distributed book of all time.
- **66 Books** in the Old and New Testament of the Bible.
- **40+ Authors.** Written by more than 40 authors, including kings, prophets, poets, musicians, and fisherman[2]
- **1,000+ Years.** Written over a span of 1,000 or more years[3]
- **3 Original Languages.** Originally written in 3 languages: Hebrew, Greek, Aramaic[4]
- **2,454 Translated Languages.** Translated into 2,454 languages of the world's estimated 6,500 total languages[5]
- It is commonly believed that the authors of the Bible were inspired by God
- Bible books include letters, poetry, songs, legal documentation, eyewitness accounts, biographies, historical literature and documents[6]

Common phrases originating from the Bible
- "Let there be light" Genesis 1:3
- "Am I my brother's keeper?" Genesis 4:9
- "fire and brimstone" Psalms 11:6
- "Eye for eye, tooth for tooth" Exodus 21:24
- "Blind leading the blind" Matthew 15:14
- "eat, drink, and be merry" Luke 12:19
- " as a lamb to the slaughter" Isaiah 53:7
- "the writing is on the wall" Daniel 5:5
- "scapegoat" Leviticus 16:10
- " at their wits' end" Psalms 107:27

The Bible is the most sold, read, bought, published, given away, believed, translated, quoted, and accurate book the world has ever experienced!

---

[1] Bible Society 1992 survey (http://www.biblesociety.org.uk/about-the-bible/what-is-the-bible/what-is-the-bible-2/ also http://www.ipl.org/div/farq/bestsellerFARQ.html)
[2] Ibid.
[3] Bible Society (http://www.biblesociety.org.uk/about-the-bible/what-is-the-bible/what-is-the-bible-2/)
[4] http://www.christiancourier.com/articles/200-languages-of-the-bible
[5] United Bible Societies (http://www.unitedbiblesocieties.org/?page_id=2)
[6] Ibid.

OLD TESTAMENT

GENESIS

Overview:

Genesis tells the story of God's creation of the world including Adam & Eve and their sin. It follows the lineage of Adam to Noah and then to Abraham and his descendants, including Isaac, Jacob, and Joseph. It emphasizes the themes of creation, sin, faith, and God's sovereignty.

Presumed Author:

> Moses

Estimated Date Written:

> 1400 B.C.

Key Events:

- The Creation (chapters 1-2)
- Adam & Eve and descendants (chapters 2-4)
- Noah and the flood (chapters 6-7)
- Tower of Babel (chapter 11)
- Abraham & Family (chapters 11-25)
- Sodom & Gomorrah (chapter 18)
- Isaac (chapters 25-26)
- Jacob (chapters 27-35)
- Esau and family (chapter 36)
- Joseph (chapters 37-50)

Key Themes:

- Creation and the nature of God
- Sin and its consequences
- Covenants and promises

Key verse(s):

"In the beginning God created the heaven and the earth."
Genesis 1:1 KJV

EXODUS

Overview:
The book of Exodus tells the story of how God delivered the Israelites from slavery in Egypt and led them to the Promised Land.

Presumed Author:
Moses

Estimated date written:
1400 B.C.

Key events:
- Life of Moses (chapters 1-2)
- God appears to Moses in the burning bush and calls him to lead the Israelites out of Egypt (chapters 3-4)
- Moses and his brother Aaron confront Pharaoh and demand that he let the Israelites go (chapters 5-12)
- 10 plagues of Egypt, culminating in the death of the firstborn (chapters 7-12)
- The Israelites leave Egypt and cross the Red Sea (chapters 13-14)
- The giving of the Ten Commandments on Mount Sinai (chapters 19-20)
- The construction of the tabernacle, a portable sanctuary for worship (chapters 25-31, 35-40)

Key themes:
- God's faithfulness to his promises to Abraham, Isaac, and Jacob
- God's power to deliver his people from slavery
- The importance of obedience to God's commands
- The establishment of the Mosaic covenant between God and the Israelites
- The role of the priesthood and the tabernacle in worship and atonement for sin

Key verse(s):

"And God said unto Moses, I AM THAT I AM: and he said, Thus shalt thou say unto the children of Israel, I AM hath sent me unto you." Exodus 3:14 KJV

"Thou shalt have no other gods before me." Exodus 20:3 KJV

LEVITICUS

Overview:
This book contains laws and instructions given by God to the Israelites regarding worship, offerings, and the priesthood. It emphasizes the themes of holiness, sacrifice, and obedience to God.

Presumed Author:
Moses

Estimated date written:
1400 B.C.

Key events:
- Laws regarding burnt offerings, grain offerings, and peace offerings (chapter 1-3)
- The consecration of Aaron and his sons as priests (chapter 8)
- Laws regarding clean and unclean animals and purification rituals (chapter 11-15)
- The Day of Atonement and the scapegoat ritual (chapter 16)
- Laws regarding sexual morality, including prohibitions against incest, adultery, and homosexual acts (chapter 18)
- The Jubilee year and the redemption of property (chapter 25)
- Blessings and curses for obedience and disobedience to God's commands (chapter 26)

Key themes:
- The holiness of God and importance of obedience to God's commands
- The role of sacrifice and offerings in worship and atonement for sin
- The establishment of the priesthood and the Levites' role in assisting them
- The distinction between clean and unclean animals, foods, and people

Key verse(s):

"And I will walk among you, and will be your God, and ye shall be my people." Leviticus 26:12 KJV

"Ye shall not make any cuttings in your flesh for the dead, nor print any marks upon you: I am the LORD." Leviticus 19:28 KJV

NUMBERS

Overview:

This book tells the story of the Israelites' journey from Mount Sinai to the border of the Promised Land, including their rebellion against God, their wandering in the wilderness, and their preparation for battle. It emphasizes the themes of faith, obedience, and God's provision.

Presumed Author:

Moses

Estimated date written:

1400 B.C.

Key events:

- The census of the Israelites (chapter 1-4)
- The rebellion of Korah and his followers (chapter 16)
- The sending of the spies into the Promised Land and their report (chapter 13-14)
- The rebellion of the Israelites and God's punishment of them (chapter 11-12, 14)
- The story of Balaam and his talking donkey (chapter 22-24)
- The defeat of the Midianites and the distribution of the spoils of war (chapter 31)
- The appointment of Joshua as Moses' successor (chapter 27)

Key themes:

- The importance of faith and obedience to God
- The consequences of rebellion and disobedience
- The role of the Levites in the worship and service of the tabernacle
- The Israelites' struggles with faith and trust in God

Key verse(s):

"The LORD bless thee, and keep thee: The LORD make his face shine upon thee, and be gracious unto thee: The LORD lift up his countenance upon thee, and give thee peace."
Numbers 6:24-26 KJV

DEUTERONOMY

Overview:
This book contains Moses' final speeches to the Israelites before they enter the Promised Land, including a restatement of the law and a call to love and obey God. It emphasizes the themes of covenant, obedience, and blessing and curse.

Presumed Author:
>   Moses

Estimated date written:
>   1400 B.C.

Key events:
- Call to love God with all your heart, soul, and strength (Chapter 6)
- Blessings and curses of the covenant (Chapter 28)
- Choice between life and death (Chapter 30)
- Death of Moses (Chapter 34)

Key themes:
- The importance of obedience to God's commands
- The covenant relationship between God and Israel
- The call to love and worship God alone

Key verse(s):

"And thou shalt love the LORD thy God with all thine heart, and with all thy soul, and with all thy might." Deuteronomy 6:5 KJV

"Be strong and of a good courage, fear not, nor be afraid of them: for the LORD thy God, he it is that doth go with thee; he will not fail thee, nor forsake thee." Deuteronomy 31:6 KJV

"And thou shalt teach them diligently unto thy children, and shalt talk of them when thou sittest in thine house, and when thou walkest by the way, and when thou liest down, and when thou risest up." Deuteronomy 6:7 KJV

JOSHUA

Overview:
This book tells the story of the Israelites' conquest of the Promised Land under the leadership of Joshua. It emphasizes the themes of faith, courage, and the faithfulness of God.

Presumed Author:
> Joshua

Estimated date written:
> 1350 B.C.

Key events:
- God commissions Joshua to lead the Israelites into the Promised Land (Chapter 1)
- The fall of Jericho (Chapter 6)
- Joshua's farewell address and the renewal of the covenant (Chapter 24)

Key themes:
- The conquest of the Promised Land
- The importance of obedience to God's commands
- The role of faith and courage in the face of challenges and opposition

Key verse(s):

"Have not I commanded thee? Be strong and of a good courage; be not afraid, neither be thou dismayed: for the LORD thy God is with thee whithersoever thou goest." Joshua 1:9 KJV

"...as for me and my house, we will serve the LORD." Joshua 24:15 KJV

JUDGES

Overview:
This book contains stories of the Israelites' repeated cycles of sin, judgment, and deliverance by various judges raised up by God. It emphasizes the themes of sin, repentance, and God's mercy.

Presumed Author:

Various authors including Samuel/Nathan/Gad

Estimated date written:

1000 - 900 B.C.

Key events:

- Othniel delivers Israel from the king of Mesopotamia - Judges 3:7-11
- Deborah and Barak lead Israel in battle against the Canaanites - Judges 4-5
- Gideon defeats the Midianites with just 300 men, but later creates an ephod that becomes a snare to him and his family - Judges 6-8
- Abimelech, Gideon's son, kills his brothers and becomes a wicked ruler over Israel - Judges 9
- Jephthah defeats the Ammonites in battle but foolishly vows to sacrifice the first thing that comes out of his house, leading to the death of his daughter - Judges 10-12
- Samson, a Nazirite with supernatural strength, defeats the Philistines but falls in love with a Philistine woman named Delilah, who betrays him to the Philistines - Judges 13-16
- The tribe of Benjamin is nearly wiped out by a civil war - Judges 19-21

Key themes:

- Idolatry: Israel repeatedly fell into idolatry and worshipped false gods
- Cycle of Sin: Israel follows a pattern of sinning, punishment, crying out, and being delivered.

Key verse(s):

"That the LORD sent a prophet unto the children of Israel, which said unto them, Thus saith the LORD God of Israel, I brought you up from Egypt, and brought you forth out of the house of bondage;" Judges 6:8 KJV

RUTH

Overview:

This book tells the story of Ruth, a Moabite woman who becomes a follower of the God of Israel and marries Boaz, a wealthy landowner. It emphasizes the themes of loyalty, faithfulness, and God's provision.

Presumed Author:

Various authors including Samuel/Nathan/Gad

Estimated date written:

1000 - 900 B.C.

Key events:

- Naomi and her family move to Moab to escape a famine in Israel. Naomi's husband and sons die, leaving her with her two daughters-in-law, Ruth and Orpah.
- Ruth and Naomi return to Israel and Ruth begins gleaning in Boaz's fields to provide for herself and Naomi.
- Boaz and Ruth marry, and Ruth gives birth to a son named Obed.
- Obed becomes the father of Jesse, and Jesse becomes the father of King David.

Key themes:

- Loyalty: The book of Ruth is a story of loyalty and faithfulness, as Ruth chooses to stay with Naomi and follow her God even when it would be easier to return to her own people and gods.
- Redemption: Boaz serves as a kinsman-redeemer, fulfilling the role of a family member who can buy back property and marry a widow in order to preserve the family line. This serves as a picture of God's redemption of His people.
- God's Providence: Throughout the book, it is clear that God is working behind the scenes to bring about His purposes, even in the midst of difficult circumstances and personal tragedies.

Key verse(s):

"And Ruth said, Intreat me not to leave thee, or to return from following after thee: for whither thou goest, I will go; and where thou lodgest, I will lodge: thy people shall be my people, and thy God my God:" Ruth 1:16 KJV

1 SAMUEL

Overview:

This book tells the story of the prophet Samuel, the first king of Israel (Saul), and David, who becomes Saul's successor. It emphasizes the themes of obedience, faith, and God's choice of a king.

Presumed Author:

Various authors including Samuel/Nathan/Gad

Estimated date written:

1000 - 900 B.C.

Key events:

- The book begins with the birth and early life of Samuel, who becomes a prophet and judge of Israel.
- The people of Israel demand a king, and God chooses Saul to be the first king. Saul has some military successes but also disobeys God and is rejected as king.
- God chooses David, a shepherd boy, to be the next king and he becomes Saul's loyal servant and later his enemy.

- David becomes king after Saul's death and establishes the kingdom of Israel.

Key themes:
- The book begins with the birth and early life of Samuel, who becomes a prophet and judge of Israel.
- The people of Israel demand a king, and God chooses Saul to be the first king. Saul has some military successes but also disobeys God and is rejected as king.
- God chooses David, a shepherd boy, to be the next king and he becomes Saul's loyal servant and later his enemy.
- David becomes king after Saul's death and establishes the kingdom of Israel.

Key verse(s):

"There is none holy as the LORD: for there is none beside thee: neither is there any rock like our God." 1 Samuel 2:2 KJV

2 SAMUEL

Overview:

This book continues the story of David's reign, including his conquests, his sin with Bathsheba, and his eventual decline. It emphasizes the themes of repentance, forgiveness, and the sovereignty of God.

Presumed Author:
Various authors including Samuel/Nathan/Gad

Estimated date written:
1000 - 900 B.C.

Key events:
- David is anointed as king over Judah (2 Samuel 2)
- Ish-bosheth, Saul's son, becomes king over the rest of Israel (2 Samuel 2)
- Abner, commander of Saul's army, is killed by Joab, David's commander (2 Samuel 3)
- David becomes king over all of Israel (2 Samuel 5)
- David brings the ark of the covenant to Jerusalem (2 Samuel 6)
- David commits adultery with Bathsheba and arranges for her husband, Uriah, to be killed in battle (2 Samuel 11)
- Nathan confronts David about his sin (2 Samuel 12)
- Absalom, David's son, rebels against him and tries to take the throne (2 Samuel 15-18)
- David mourns the death of Absalom (2 Samuel 18-19)
- Sheba rebels against David (2 Samuel 20)

Key themes:

- The book of 2 Samuel is primarily about David's reign as king over Israel, and his rise to power. It shows the qualities of a good king, such as humility, faithfulness, and reliance on God. It also highlights the dangers of a king who is driven by pride and self-interest, as seen in David's sin with Bathsheba and his handling of Absalom's rebellion.

Key verse(s):

"God is my strength and power: and he maketh my way perfect." 2 Samuel 22:33 KJV

1 KINGS

Overview:
This book tells the story of the reigns of King Solomon and his successors, including the division of the kingdom into Israel (the northern kingdom) and Judah (the southern kingdom). It emphasizes the themes of wisdom, faithfulness, and the consequences of sin.

Presumed Author:
Jeremiah

Estimated date written:
600 B.C.

Key events:
- Solomon becomes king after David's death (1 Kings 1-2)
- Solomon asks for wisdom from God and is granted great wealth and power (1 Kings 3-4)
- Solomon builds the temple in Jerusalem (1 Kings 5-8)
- Solomon marries many foreign women and turns away from God (1 Kings 11)
- The kingdom of Israel splits into two after Solomon's death, with Jeroboam ruling over the northern kingdom of Israel and Rehoboam ruling over the southern kingdom of Judah (1 Kings 12)
- Elijah confronts the prophets of Baal on Mount Carmel (1 Kings 18)
- Elijah flees from Queen Jezebel and encounters God on Mount Horeb (1 Kings 19)
- Ahab and Jezebel's sins lead to the downfall of their dynasty and the rise of Jehu as king (1 Kings 21-22)

Key themes:

The book of 1 Kings focuses on the reigns of the kings of Israel and Judah, and their successes and failures in following God's commands. It shows the importance of wise and faithful leadership, as well as the consequences of disobedience and idolatry.

Key verse(s):

"The LORD our God be with us, as he was with our fathers: let him not leave us, nor forsake us:" 1 Kings 8:57 KJV

2 KINGS

Overview:
This book continues the story of the kings of Israel and Judah, including the fall of both kingdoms to Assyria and Babylon, respectively. It emphasizes the themes of judgment, faithfulness, and the consequences of disobedience.

Presumed Author:
Jeremiah

Estimated date written:
600 B.C.

Key events:
- Elijah is taken up into heaven in a whirlwind (2 Kings 2)
- Elisha becomes the prophet of Israel and performs miracles (2 Kings 2-8)
- Jehu becomes king of Israel and kills the family of Ahab (2 Kings 9-10)
- Assyria conquers Israel and takes the people into exile (2 Kings 17)
- Josiah becomes king of Judah and institutes religious reforms (2 Kings 22-23)
- Babylon conquers Judah and destroys the temple in Jerusalem (2 Kings 24-25)

Key themes:
The book of 2 Kings continues the theme of the prophetic tradition that was established in 1 Kings. The prophets play an important role in guiding the kings and people of Israel and Judah, and in warning them of the consequences of their actions.

Key verse(s):

"And he answered, Fear not: for they that be with us are more than they that be with them." 2 Kings 6:16 KJV

1 CHRONICLES

Overview:

This book is a genealogy of the Israelite people from Adam to King David, with an emphasis on the lineage of David. It emphasizes the themes of faithfulness, obedience, and God's plan.

Presumed Author:

Ezra

Estimated date written:

450 B.C.

Key events:

- Genealogies of Adam to David (1 Chronicles 1-9)
- David becomes king of Israel and conquers Jerusalem (1 Chronicles 10-11)
- David brings the ark of the covenant to Jerusalem and plans to build the temple (1 Chronicles 13-17)
- David's military victories and conquests (1 Chronicles 18-20)
- David's sin with Bathsheba and his repentance (1 Chronicles 21-22)
- David instructs Solomon to build the temple and prepares for his own death (1 Chronicles 28-29)

Key themes:

- Genealogy
- The Davidic Covenant
- Worship
- Repentance and Forgiveness
- Faithfulness to God's Commands

Key verse(s):

"Seek the LORD and his strength, seek his face continually." 1 Chronicles 16:11 KJV

2 CHRONICLES

Overview:

This book continues the story of the kings of Judah, focusing on the reigns of several good and bad kings, and ends with the exile to Babylon. It emphasizes the themes of faithfulness, repentance, and God's sovereignty.

Presumed Author:

Ezra

Estimated date written:

450 B.C.

Key events:

- Solomon becomes king of Israel and builds the temple in Jerusalem (2 Chronicles 1-7)
- The division of the kingdom of Israel and Judah after Solomon's death (2 Chronicles 10)
- The reigns of the kings of Judah, including Asa, Jehoshaphat, Hezekiah, and Josiah (2 Chronicles 14-35)
- The Babylonian exile and the destruction of the temple in Jerusalem (2 Chronicles 36)

Key themes:

- Worship
- Faithfulness to God's Commands
- The Davidic Covenant
- Divine Judgment and Mercy
- The Importance of Repentance

Key verse(s):

"If my people, which are called by my name, shall humble themselves, and pray, and seek my face, and turn from their wicked ways; then will I hear from heaven, and will forgive their sin, and will heal their land." 2 Chronicles 7:14 KJV

EZRA

Overview:
This book tells the story of the Israelites' return from exile in Babylon and the rebuilding of the temple in Jerusalem. It emphasizes the themes of repentance, restoration, and God's faithfulness.

Presumed Author:
Ezra

Estimated date written:
450 B.C.

Key events:
- The decree of Cyrus allowing the Jews to return to Jerusalem and rebuild the temple (Ezra 1)
- The return of the exiles led by Zerubbabel and Joshua, and the rebuilding of the altar and temple (Ezra 2-6)
- The arrival of Ezra in Jerusalem and his efforts to teach the Law to the people and promote religious reforms (Ezra 7-10)

Key themes:
- Restoration: The book of Ezra emphasizes the restoration of the Jewish people and their return to Jerusalem after their exile in Babylon.
- Rebuilding: The book of Ezra highlights the physical rebuilding of the temple in Jerusalem and the spiritual rebuilding of the Jewish community.
- Law: The book of Ezra emphasizes the importance of the Law of Moses, particularly in the context of Ezra's efforts to teach it to the people and promote religious reforms.
- Repentance: The book of Ezra emphasizes the importance of repentance and turning back to God, particularly in the context of Ezra's call for the people to confess their sins and seek forgiveness.
- Grace and Mercy: The book of Ezra highlights the grace and mercy of God in allowing the exiles to return to Jerusalem and rebuild the temple, despite their past disobedience.

Key verse(s):

"For I was ashamed to require of the king a band of soldiers and horsemen to help us against the enemy in the way: because we had spoken unto the king, saying, The hand of our God is upon all them for good that seek him; but his power and his wrath is against all them that forsake him." Ezra 8:22 KJV

NEHEMIAH

Overview:

This book tells the story of Nehemiah, a cupbearer to the Persian king who leads the rebuilding of the walls of Jerusalem and helps the Israelites return to their covenant with God. It emphasizes the themes of leadership, faithfulness, and restoration.

Presumed Author:

Ezra

Estimated date written:

450 B.C.

Key events:

- Nehemiah's commission to return to Jerusalem and rebuild the city walls (Nehemiah 1-2)
- The opposition and challenges faced by Nehemiah and the people in rebuilding the walls (Nehemiah 4-6)
- The renewal of the covenant and dedication of the rebuilt walls (Nehemiah 8-12)
- Nehemiah's reforms, including the restoration of the Sabbath and the purification of the priesthood (Nehemiah 13)

Key themes:

- Leadership: The book of Nehemiah emphasizes the importance of strong and effective leadership, particularly in the context of Nehemiah's efforts to rebuild the city walls and promote religious reforms. It highlights prayer, courage, and determination.
- Rebuilding: The book of Nehemiah focuses on the physical rebuilding of Jerusalem's walls, but it also emphasizes the spiritual rebuilding of the Jewish community.
- Opposition and Perseverance: The book of Nehemiah shows the challenges and opposition faced by Nehemiah and the people in rebuilding the city walls.
- Confession and Repentance: The book of Nehemiah highlights the importance of confession and repentance, particularly in the context of the people's recognition of their past disobedience and the need to renew their covenant with God.
- Sabbath and Worship: The book of Nehemiah emphasizes the importance of Sabbath rest and worship, particularly in the context of Nehemiah's efforts to promote religious reforms.

Key verse(s):

"Then he said unto them, Go your way, eat the fat, and drink the sweet, and send portions unto them for whom nothing is prepared: for this day is holy unto our Lord: neither be ye sorry; for the joy of the LORD is your strength." Nehemiah 8:10 KJV

ESTHER

Overview:

This book tells the story of Esther, a Jewish woman who becomes queen of Persia and saves her people from a plot to destroy them. It emphasizes the themes of courage, faithfulness, and God's sovereignty.

Presumed Author:

Mordecai

Estimated date written:

400 B.C.

Key events:

- King Xerxes of Persia holds a lavish banquet and orders Queen Vashti to appear before him. When she refuses, he banishes her and begins the search for a new queen (Esther 1).
- Esther, a Jewish woman, is selected as the new queen and conceals her identity at the urging of her cousin Mordecai (Esther 2).
- Haman, an influential official in Xerxes' court, becomes enraged when Mordecai refuses to bow down to him and plots to have all the Jews in the empire killed (Esther 3).
- Esther reveals her Jewish identity to Xerxes and pleads for him to spare her people. Xerxes agrees and Haman is executed (Esther 4-8).
- The Jews defend themselves against their attackers and celebrate their victory with the holiday of Purim (Esther 9-10).

Key themes:

- Providence: The book of Esther shows how God can work behind the scenes to bring about his purposes even in the midst of seemingly random or chance events.
- Identity: Esther's concealment of her Jewish identity and eventual revelation of it highlights the importance of knowing and embracing one's identity.
- Courage: Esther's willingness to risk her life by revealing her identity and pleading for her people demonstrates the courage required to stand up for what is right.
- Faithfulness: Mordecai's refusal to bow down to Haman and Esther's willingness to risk her life for her people illustrate the importance of faithfulness to God and one's community.

Key verse(s):

> "For if thou altogether holdest thy peace at this time, then shall there enlargement and deliverance arise to the Jews from another place; but thou and thy father's house shall be destroyed: and who knoweth whether thou art come to the kingdom for such a time as this?"
> Esther 4:14 KJV

JOB

Overview:
This book tells the story of Job, a righteous man who suffers great loss and affliction, and his conversations with his friends and with God about the nature of suffering and the character of God. It emphasizes the themes of faithfulness, perseverance, and God's wisdom.

Presumed Author:
Moses

Estimated date written:
1400 B.C.

Key events:
- Job, a wealthy and righteous man, is tested by Satan, who takes away his possessions, kills his children, and afflicts him with painful sores (Job 1-2).
- Job's three friends come to comfort him, but they argue that his suffering must be due to some sin or wrongdoing on his part (Job 3-37).
- Job challenges his friends' accusations and laments his suffering, expressing his confusion and despair (Job 38-42).
- God speaks to Job, affirming his sovereignty and wisdom and calling Job to trust in him (Job 38-41).
- Job repents of his questioning of God and is restored, receiving twice as much wealth as before (Job 42).

Key themes:
- Suffering: The book of Job wrestles with the question of why the righteous suffer. It shows that suffering can come to anyone, regardless of their righteousness, and that it can be a test of faith and an opportunity for growth.
- Faith: Job's faith is tested by his suffering, but he remains steadfast, even when his friends accuse him of wrongdoing. His faithfulness is ultimately vindicated by God.
- Restoration: Job's restoration at the end of the book shows that God can bring good out of even the most difficult circumstances and that he rewards those who trust in him.

Key verse(s):

"For I know that my redeemer liveth, and that he shall stand at the latter day upon the earth:"
Job 19:25 KJV

PSALMS

Overview:
This book is a collection of 150 poetic and lyrical songs, prayers, and meditations that were likely used in worship services in ancient Israel. Many of the Psalms were written by King David and others by unknown authors, which cover a wide range of themes: from praise and thanksgiving to lament and supplication.

Presumed Author:
Various authors (mostly David)

Estimated date written:
1000 - 400 B.C.

Key events:
- The book of Psalms is a collection of 150 individual songs and poems, written by various authors over a period of centuries.
- Many of the psalms are attributed to King David, who was known for his musical and poetic abilities.
- The psalms cover a wide range of themes and emotions, including praise and worship, thanksgiving, confession, lament, and supplication.
- Some of the psalms are accompanied by musical notations indicating the instruments to be used and the style of singing.

Key themes:
- Worship: The book of Psalms is primarily a book of worship and contains numerous hymns of praise and thanksgiving to God.
- Prayer: Many of the psalms are prayers, expressing the author's desires, concerns, and emotions to God. They show the importance of prayer as a means of communication with God.
- Wisdom: The book of Psalms contains many proverbs and sayings that offer wisdom for living, such as the importance of trusting in God, seeking righteousness, and avoiding evil.
- Justice: The psalms frequently speak of God's justice and call for the punishment of the wicked and the protection of the innocent.
- Messiah: The book of Psalms contains several prophecies and references to the coming Messiah, who would bring hope of redemption and salvation.

Key verse(s):

"And he shall be like a tree planted by the rivers of water, that bringeth forth his fruit in his season; his leaf also shall not wither; and whatsoever he doeth shall prosper." Psalms 1:3 KJV

PROVERBS

Overview:

This book is a collection of wise sayings and teachings attributed to King Solomon, as well as other wise individuals in Israelite society. The proverbs cover a wide range of topics, from relationships and parenting to business and politics, and emphasize the importance of living a virtuous and Godly life.

Presumed Author:

Solomon

Estimated date written:

900 B.C.

Key events:

- Solomon, as well as other wise men of Israel.
- The sayings cover a range of topics, including wisdom, righteousness, family life, friendship, wealth, and speech.
- The sayings are often written in short, memorable phrases or couplets, making them easy to remember and apply to daily life.
- The book of Proverbs is designed to provide practical guidance for wise living and to help the reader gain understanding and discernment.

Key themes:

- Wisdom: The book of Proverbs emphasizes the importance of wisdom and understanding for living a successful and fulfilling life.
- Character: The proverbs frequently address the importance of character traits such as honesty, diligence, humility, and self-control. They encourage the reader to cultivate these traits and avoid their opposites.
- Relationships: The proverbs offer guidance for building healthy relationships, including friendships, family relationships, and romantic relationships.
- Speech: The proverbs frequently address the power of words and the importance of using speech wisely. They encourage the reader to speak truthfully and kindly, and to avoid gossip and slander.

Key verse(s):

"The fear of the LORD is the beginning of knowledge: but fools despise wisdom and instruction." Proverbs 1:7 KJV

ECCLESIASTES

Overview:

This book is a philosophical reflection on the meaning of life, written by an author who identifies himself as "the Teacher." The book explores the futility of human pursuits and the inevitability of death, but ultimately affirms the value of finding joy in the present moment and living in obedience to God.

Presumed Author:

Solomon

Estimated date written:

900 B.C.

Key events:

- The book of Ecclesiastes is written by an author referred to as "the Teacher" or "the Preacher."
- The author reflects on the futility and meaninglessness of life, and the struggle to find satisfaction and purpose in the midst of life's challenges and uncertainties.
- The author describes various pursuits and pleasures, such as wealth, wisdom, and pleasure, but ultimately concludes that they are all meaningless and temporary.
- The author encourages the reader to fear God and to enjoy life's simple pleasures, such as food, drink, and companionship.

Key themes:

- Vanity: The book of Ecclesiastes is known for its repeated refrain, "vanity of vanities; all is vanity." The author reflects on the fleeting and temporary nature of life and the pursuit of worldly pleasures, and concludes that they are ultimately meaningless and empty.
- Wisdom: Despite his pessimistic view of life, the author recognizes the value of wisdom and knowledge. He encourages the reader to seek wisdom, but also acknowledges that wisdom alone cannot provide ultimate satisfaction or meaning in life.
- Time: The book of Ecclesiastes emphasizes the importance of time and the fleeting nature of life. The author encourages the reader to use their time wisely and to enjoy life's simple pleasures while they can.

Key verse(s):

"Let us hear the conclusion of the whole matter: Fear God, and keep his commandments: for this is the whole duty of man." Ecclesiastes 12:13 KJV

SONG OF SOLOMON

Overview:

This book is a collection of love poems that celebrate the joys of romantic and sexual love, often using vivid and sensual imagery. The book is traditionally interpreted as an allegory of God's love for Israel or Christ's love for the Church, but many modern scholars see it as a celebration of human love in its own right.

Presumed Author:

Solomon

Estimated date written:

900 B.C.

Key events:

- The book of Song of Solomon (also known as Song of Songs) is a collection of love poems or songs that celebrate the beauty and intimacy of romantic love between a man and a woman.
- The book contains dialogue between a man and a woman, and describes their love for each other in sensual and poetic language.
- The identity of the man and woman in the poems is not specified, but they are generally understood to represent a husband and wife or a young couple in love.
- The poems touch on themes such as attraction, courtship, marriage, and physical intimacy.

Key themes:

- Love: The book of Song of Solomon celebrates the beauty and power of romantic love between a man and a woman. The poems use poetic and sensual language to describe the physical and emotional aspects of romantic love.
- Courtship: The poems also touch on the process of courtship and the development of a romantic relationship.
- Marriage: The book of Song of Solomon also celebrates the institution of marriage and the intimacy that it brings.
- God's Love: Some interpreters see the book of Song of Solomon as an allegory for the love between God and his people. They see the poems as describing the passionate love and intimacy that God desires to have with his people.

Key verse(s):

"He brought me to the banqueting house, and his banner over me was love." Song of Solomon 2:4 KJV

ISAIAH

Overview:
This book is a prophetic work that contains a mix of warnings, encouragements, and messages of hope for the nation of Israel. The prophet Isaiah speaks to the people during a time of great political turmoil and calls on them to repent of their sins and turn back to God. The book also contains many prophecies of a future Messiah who will come to save Israel and usher in a new era of peace and justice.

Presumed Author:
Isaiah

Estimated date written:
700 B.C.

Key events:
- Isaiah prophesied during a time of political and social upheaval in Judah, as the nation faced threats from Assyria and Babylon.
- The book is divided into two main sections: chapters 1-39 contain prophecies related to Judah and its surrounding nations, while chapters 40-66 contain prophecies of comfort and restoration for the exiles in Babylon.

Key themes:
- Holiness of God: The book of Isaiah emphasizes the holiness and majesty of God. Isaiah sees a vision of God in the temple, and his prophecies often reflect a sense of awe and reverence for God's greatness.
- Messiah: a coming Messiah is prophesied who will be a descendant of David and will reign in righteousness and justice. It mentions a "Servant of the Lord," who will suffer and be rejected but will ultimately bring salvation to God's people. These prophecies point forward to the coming of Jesus Christ.
- Restoration and Hope: Despite the warnings of judgment, Isaiah also prophesies about a coming restoration and hope for God's people- a new Jerusalem and a new creation.

Key verse(s):

"For unto us a child is born, unto us a son is given: and the government shall be upon his shoulder: and his name shall be called Wonderful, Counsellor, The mighty God, The everlasting Father, The Prince of Peace." Isaiah 9:6 KJV

JEREMIAH

Overview:

This book is a collection of prophecies and narratives that center around the life and ministry of the prophet Jeremiah. Jeremiah prophesies during a time of great political upheaval, warning the people of Israel to repent before it is too late. The book also contains many passages of personal reflection and lament from the prophet himself.

Presumed Author:

Jeremiah

Estimated date written:

600 B.C.

Key events:

- The book of Jeremiah is named after the prophet Jeremiah, who lived in the southern kingdom of Judah during the sixth century BC.
- Jeremiah prophesied during a time of political and social turmoil in Judah, as the nation faced threats from Babylon and internal corruption and idolatry.
- Jeremiah's prophecies contain warnings of judgment and calls to repentance, as well as promises of restoration and hope.
- The book is divided into two main sections: chapters 1-25 contain prophecies related to Judah and its impending judgment, while chapters 26-52 contain historical accounts of Jeremiah's ministry and the fall of Jerusalem to Babylon.

Key themes:

- Covenant and Judgment: Jeremiah prophesies judgment upon Judah for its rebellion against God and its failure to uphold its covenant responsibilities.
- Repentance and Restoration: Despite the warnings of judgment, Jeremiah also offers a message of hope and restoration for God's people.
- False Prophets: Throughout the book, Jeremiah encounters false prophets who offer false hope and security to the people of Judah.
- Suffering: Jeremiah's own life is marked by suffering and rejection, and his prophecies often contain themes of suffering and persecution for God's people. He points forward to the coming of a suffering servant who will ultimately bring salvation to God's people.

Key verse(s):

"Before I formed thee in the belly I knew thee; and before thou camest forth out of the womb I sanctified thee, and I ordained thee a prophet unto the nations." Jeremiah 1:5 KJV

LAMENTATIONS

Overview:
This book is a series of poetic laments over the destruction of Jerusalem and the Babylonian exile. The book is traditionally attributed to the prophet Jeremiah and is written in an acrostic format, with each chapter beginning with a successive letter of the Hebrew alphabet.

Presumed Author:
Jeremiah

Estimated date written:
600 B.C.

Key events:
- The book of Lamentations is a collection of five poems or laments mourning the destruction of Jerusalem and the temple by the Babylonians in 586 BC.
- The author of Lamentations is unknown, but the poems are traditionally attributed to the prophet Jeremiah.
- The poems express deep sorrow, grief, and lament over the destruction of the city and the suffering of its people, as well as a confession of sin and a plea for mercy from God.

Key themes:
- Sorrow and Mourning: The primary theme of Lamentations is sorrow and mourning over the destruction of Jerusalem and the suffering of its people. The poems express deep emotional pain and lament the loss of the city, the temple, and the people's way of life.
- Sin and Repentance: The author of Lamentations recognizes that the destruction of Jerusalem was a result of the people's sin and rebellion against God.
- God's Judgment and Mercy: The author of Lamentations recognizes that the destruction of Jerusalem was a result of God's judgment upon the people's sin.
- Community and Solidarity: The poems of Lamentations express a sense of communal mourning and solidarity among the people of Jerusalem.
- Hope in God: Despite the deep sorrow and grief expressed in the poems, Lamentations also contains a message of hope in God's faithfulness and his promise to restore his people.

Key verse(s):

"It is of the LORD'S mercies that we are not consumed, because his compassions fail not."
Lamentations 3:22 KJV

EZEKIEL

Overview:
This book contains a series of prophetic visions and oracles delivered by the prophet Ezekiel, who was himself a priest and was exiled to Babylon along with many other Israelites. The book contains many vivid and symbolic images, including the famous vision of the "valley of dry bones" that is interpreted as a symbol of Israel's spiritual renewal.

Presumed Author:
Ezekiel

Estimated date written:
550 B.C.

Key events:
- The book of Ezekiel is named after the prophet Ezekiel, who was taken into captivity in Babylon in 597 BC along with King Jehoiachin and many other Judean leaders.
- Ezekiel prophesied to the exiled community of Judeans in Babylon, delivering messages of warning, judgment, and hope.
- The book contains a number of vivid symbolic visions and actions, including the famous vision of the valley of dry bones in chapter 37.
- Ezekiel's prophecies include judgments against other nations as well as against Judah, and he also prophesies about the coming of a new temple and a new covenant with God.

Key themes:
- Holiness and Idolatry: The book of Ezekiel emphasizes holiness and the dangers of idolatry.
- Judgment and Restoration: Ezekiel's prophecies contain both warnings of judgment for Judah and other nations and promises of restoration and hope.
- Faithfulness of God: The book of Ezekiel emphasizes the faithfulness of God to his people, even in the midst of their sin and rebellion.
- Responsibility and Accountability: Ezekiel's prophecies emphasize the importance of individual responsibility and accountability for one's actions.
- Vision and Symbolism: The book of Ezekiel contains many vivid symbolic visions and actions, which serve to illustrate Ezekiel's messages and to convey the reality of God's presence and power.

Key verse(s):

"A new heart also will I give you, and a new spirit will I put within you: and I will take away the stony heart out of your flesh, and I will give you an heart of flesh." Ezekiel 36:26 KJV

DANIEL

Overview:

This book contains a series of narratives and apocalyptic visions that center around the life and ministry of the prophet Daniel, who was also exiled to Babylon. The book contains many vivid and symbolic images, including the famous vision of the "four beasts" that represent the empires of Babylon, Persia, Greece, and Rome.

Presumed Author:

Daniel

Estimated date written:

550 B.C.

Key events:

- The book of Daniel tells the story of Daniel, a young Israelite who was taken into captivity in Babylon in 605 BC along with other members of the Judean elite.
- Daniel served in the court of King Nebuchadnezzar and later in the courts of other Babylonian and Persian rulers.
- The book contains a number of prophetic visions and apocalyptic writings, including the famous vision of the four beasts in chapter 7 and the vision of the 70 weeks in chapter 9.
- The book also tells the stories of Daniel's three friends, Shadrach, Meshach, and Abednego, and their miraculous deliverance from the fiery furnace.

Key themes:

- Faithfulness and Courage: The book of Daniel emphasizes the importance of faithfulness and courage in the face of opposition and persecution in the midst of a pagan culture.
- Prophetic Vision and Apocalypticism: The book of Daniel contains a number of prophetic visions and apocalyptic writings that reveal God's plans for the future. These visions include the four beasts, the vision of the ram and the goat, and the vision of the 70 weeks.
- Sovereignty of God: The book of Daniel emphasizes the sovereignty of God over all nations and rulers.
- Interpretation of Dreams: The book of Daniel is known for its interpretation of dreams and visions. Daniel is able to interpret the dreams of Nebuchadnezzar, Belshazzar, and others, revealing their meaning and significance.

Key verse(s):

"Then was the king exceeding glad for him, and commanded that they should take Daniel up out of the den. So Daniel was taken up out of the den, and no manner of hurt was found upon him, because he believed in his God." Daniel 6:23 KJV

PROPHESY: MINOR PROPHETS

HOSEA

Overview:

This book contains a series of prophetic messages from the prophet Hosea, who uses his own troubled marriage as a metaphor for God's relationship with Israel. Hosea calls on the people of Israel to repent and turn back to God, warning of the consequences of continued disobedience.

Presumed Author:

Hosea

Estimated date written:

750 B.C.

Key events:

- The book of Hosea is named after the prophet Hosea, who prophesied to the northern kingdom of Israel during the reigns of Jeroboam II and other kings in the 8th century BC.
- Hosea's prophecies focus on the unfaithfulness of Israel to God and the consequences of their sin.
- Hosea is instructed by God to marry a promiscuous woman named Gomer, as a symbolic representation of God's relationship with Israel.
- The book contains a number of prophetic oracles, including judgments against Israel and promises of restoration and redemption.

Key themes:

- Covenant and Unfaithfulness: The book of Hosea emphasizes the theme of covenant and unfaithfulness. Hosea uses his own marriage to Gomer as a metaphor for God's relationship with Israel, which has been marked by unfaithfulness and idolatry.
- Judgment and Mercy: Hosea's prophecies contain both warnings of judgment for Israel's sin and promises of mercy and restoration. Despite Israel's unfaithfulness, God promises to remain faithful to his covenant and to ultimately redeem his people.
- Love and Grace: The book of Hosea also emphasizes the theme of God's love and grace toward his people, despite their sin and unfaithfulness.

Key verse(s):

"Then shall we know, if we follow on to know the LORD: his going forth is prepared as the morning; and he shall come unto us as the rain, as the latter and former rain unto the earth."
Hosea 6:3 KJV

JOEL

Overview:

This book contains a series of prophetic messages from the prophet Joel, who speaks to the people of Israel during a time of great drought and locust plagues. Joel calls on the people to repent and turn back to God, promising that if they do, God will restore their fortunes and send them blessings. The book also contains prophecies about a future day of judgment and a pouring out of God's Spirit on all people.

Presumed Author:

> Joel

Estimated date written:

> 850 B.C.

Key events:

- The book of Joel is named after the prophet Joel, who prophesied to the southern kingdom of Judah in the 9th century BC.
- The book contains a series of prophetic oracles and warnings, which are primarily focused on the impending judgment of God.
- Joel prophesies a locust plague that will devastate the land, which he sees as a sign of the coming day of the Lord, a time of judgment and reckoning.
- Joel also calls for repentance and spiritual renewal, urging the people of Judah to turn back to God and seek his forgiveness.

Key themes:

- Day of the Lord: The book of Joel emphasizes the theme of the day of the Lord, a time of judgment and reckoning when God will pour out his wrath on the nations. Joel sees the impending locust plague as a sign of this coming judgment, which will ultimately lead to the restoration and renewal of God's people.
- Repentance and Renewal: Joel emphasizes the importance of repentance and spiritual renewal in the face of impending judgment.
- The Holy Spirit: Joel is also known for his prophesy about the outpouring of the Holy Spirit. He promises that God will pour out his Spirit on all people, young and old, male and female, and that this will lead to a time of spiritual renewal and prophetic vision.
- Judgment and Warning: Finally, the book of Joel also emphasizes the theme of judgment and warning.

Key verse(s):

"And it shall come to pass, that whosoever shall call on the name of the LORD shall be delivered: for in mount Zion and in Jerusalem shall be deliverance, as the LORD hath said, and in the remnant whom the LORD shall call." Joel 2:32 KJV

AMOS

Overview:

This book contains a series of prophetic messages from the prophet Amos, who speaks out against the social injustices and religious apostasy that were prevalent in Israel during his time. Amos warns that God will judge Israel for their sins, but also holds out the possibility of repentance and restoration.

Presumed Author:

Amos

Estimated date written:

750 B.C.

Key events:

- The book of Amos is named after the prophet Amos, who prophesied to the northern kingdom of Israel in the 8th century BC.
- Amos was a shepherd and farmer from Tekoa, a small village in Judah, but God called him to prophesy to the Israelites in the north.
- The book contains a series of prophetic oracles, in which Amos denounces the social and moral decay of Israel and warns of impending judgment.
- Amos specifically condemns the wealthy and powerful elites of Israel for their oppression of the poor and marginalized, and for their idolatry and disobedience to God's commands.

Key themes:

- Social Justice: The book of Amos emphasizes the importance of social justice and righteousness in the eyes of God. Amos condemns the wealthy elites of Israel for their oppression of the poor and marginalized, and for their unjust and corrupt practices.
- Judgment and Warning: Amos also warns of impending judgment for Israel's sins, and calls on the people to repent and turn back to God before it is too late. He uses vivid imagery to describe the coming day of the Lord, which will be a time of darkness and mourning for the people of Israel.
- Idolatry and Disobedience: Amos specifically denounces the idolatry and disobedience of Israel's leaders and people, accusing them of turning away from God and worshiping false gods and idols.
- The Sovereignty of God: Amos declares that God is in control of all things, and that he will judge the nations and restore his people according to his own purposes and plans.
- Restoration and Blessing: Despite the warnings of judgment, the book of Amos also contains promises of restoration and blessing for God's people.

Key verse(s):

"But let judgment run down as waters, and righteousness as a mighty stream." Amos 5:24 KJV

OBADIAH

Overview:

This book contains a short prophetic message of judgment against the nation of Edom, who had mistreated Israel during their time of distress. The message emphasizes God's justice and the ultimate triumph of Israel over their enemies.

Presumed Author:

Obadiah

Estimated date written:

600 B.C.

Key events:

- The book of Obadiah is the shortest book in the Old Testament, containing only one chapter.
- The book is a prophecy against the nation of Edom, which was located south of Judah and descended from Esau, the brother of Jacob.
- Edom had been a longstanding enemy of Judah, and had rejoiced over Judah's downfall and destruction by foreign powers.
- Obadiah prophesies that Edom will be judged and punished for their mistreatment of Judah and their arrogance and pride.

Key themes:

- Judgment: The primary theme of the book of Obadiah is judgment, as God declares that he will judge and punish Edom for their pride, arrogance, and mistreatment of Judah. This judgment is seen as a warning to all nations that oppose God and his people.
- Pride and Arrogance: Obadiah highlights the sin of pride and arrogance, which he sees as the root of Edom's mistreatment of Judah. He warns that those who exalt themselves will be brought low by God's judgment.
- Justice: Obadiah emphasizes the justice of God, who will vindicate his people and punish their oppressors. He declares that God is a righteous judge who will not let injustice go unpunished.
- Salvation: Although the book of Obadiah is primarily a prophecy of judgment, it also contains glimpses of God's salvation and mercy. Obadiah declares that there will be a remnant of God's people who will be saved and will possess the land of Edom, and he points to the ultimate victory of God's kingdom over all the nations of the earth.

Key verse(s):

"For the day of the LORD is near upon all the heathen: as thou hast done, it shall be done unto thee: thy reward shall return upon thine own head." Obadiah 1:15 KJV

JONAH

Overview:

This book tells the story of the prophet Jonah, who is called by God to preach a message of repentance to the people of Nineveh, but initially refuses to do so. After being swallowed by a great fish and spending three days in its belly, Jonah finally goes to Nineveh and delivers his message, which leads to the repentance of the people.

Presumed Author:

> Jonah

Estimated date written:

> 700 B.C.

Key events:

- God commands the prophet Jonah to go to the city of Nineveh and warn its people of God's impending judgment.
- Jonah disobeys God and tries to flee by taking a ship to Tarshish.
- God sends a great storm to stop Jonah's flight, and Jonah is thrown overboard and swallowed by a giant fish.
- After three days in the fish's belly, Jonah repents and is vomited up on the shore.
- Jonah goes to Nineveh and preaches repentance, and the people of the city turn from their evil ways and are spared from God's judgment.

Key themes:

- Repentance: The primary theme of the book of Jonah is repentance, as both Jonah and the people of Nineveh are called to turn from their sinful ways and seek God's mercy.
- God's Mercy: Although Jonah expects God to judge and destroy the wicked city of Nineveh, God shows mercy to the repentant Ninevites and spares them from judgment.
- Obedience: Jonah's disobedience and attempt to flee from God's command serve as a warning against disobedience and the dangers of running from God's will.
- Sovereignty: The book of Jonah also highlights God's sovereignty over all things, including nature, human history, and the hearts of people. God's control over the storm, the fish, and the hearts of the Ninevites all demonstrate his power and authority.
- Missions: The book of Jonah is often seen as a call to missions and evangelism, as Jonah is sent to preach the gospel to the people of Nineveh.

Key verse(s):

> "And said, I cried by reason of mine affliction unto the LORD, and he heard me; out of the belly of hell cried I, and thou heardest my voice." Jonah 2:2 KJV

MICAH

Overview:
This book contains a series of prophetic messages from the prophet Micah, who speaks out against the corruption and injustice that were prevalent in Israel during his time. Micah warns that God will judge the people for their sins, but also holds out the possibility of repentance and restoration.

Presumed Author:
Micah

Estimated date written:
700 B.C.

Key events:
- Micah prophesies during the reigns of Jotham, Ahaz, and Hezekiah, kings of Judah.
- Micah warns the people of Judah and Israel of God's coming judgment for their sins and corruption.
- Micah denounces the social injustices of his day, including the oppression of the poor and the abuse of power by the wealthy.
- Micah predicts the fall of Samaria and Jerusalem, as well as the Babylonian exile and eventual restoration of Israel.
- Micah prophesies about the coming Messiah, who will rule in righteousness and bring salvation to his people.

Key themes:
- Justice: The book of Micah emphasizes the importance of justice and righteousness in the sight of God.
- Judgment: Micah also warns of God's coming judgment against the sins of his people. He predicts the fall of Samaria and Jerusalem, as well as the Babylonian exile.
- Restoration: Despite the warnings of judgment, Micah also prophesies about the eventual restoration of God's people. He predicts that God will raise up a remnant from among the exiles and restore them to their land.
- Faithfulness: Micah emphasizes the importance of faithfulness to God and his commands. He calls on his listeners to turn from their idolatry and to put their trust in God alone.
- Sovereignty: The book of Micah also highlights God's sovereignty over all things.

Key verse(s):

"Therefore I will look unto the LORD; I will wait for the God of my salvation: my God will hear me." Micah 7:7 KJV

NAHUM

Overview:
This book contains a prophetic message of judgment against the city of Nineveh, which had repented at the preaching of Jonah but had subsequently returned to their wicked ways. The message emphasizes God's justice and the ultimate downfall of those who oppose Him.

Presumed Author:
> Nahum

Estimated date written:
> 650 B.C.

Key events:
- Nahum prophesies against the city of Nineveh, the capital of the Assyrian empire.
- Nahum predicts that God will judge Nineveh for its violence and cruelty towards other nations, including Israel.
- Nahum describes in vivid detail the destruction that will come upon Nineveh, including the flooding of the Tigris River and the invasion of the city by enemy armies.
- Nahum emphasizes that God is a jealous God who will not tolerate the worship of other gods, especially by his own people.

Key themes:
- Judgment: Nahum predicts that Nineveh will be destroyed because of its violence and cruelty towards others, especially Israel.
- Justice: Along with judgment, Nahum also emphasizes the justice of God. Nahum's prophecy against Nineveh is an example of God's justice, as he punishes the city for its sins.
- Sovereignty: The book of Nahum also highlights God's sovereignty over all things.
- Faithfulness: Nahum also emphasizes the faithfulness of God to his people.
- Worship: Nahum also emphasizes the importance of worshiping the true God. He warns against the worship of other gods, especially by God's own people.

Key verse(s):

"The LORD is good, a strong hold in the day of trouble; and he knoweth them that trust in him." Nahum 1:7 KJV

HABAKKUK

Overview:
This book contains a dialogue between the prophet Habakkuk and God, in which Habakkuk questions why God allows evil and injustice to go unpunished. God responds by affirming His sovereignty and justice, and promising that the righteous will live by faith.

Presumed Author:
>   Habakkuk

Estimated date written:
>   600 B.C.

Key events:
*   Habakkuk questions God's justice in light of the wickedness and violence in the world.
*   God responds to Habakkuk's questions, assuring him that he will ultimately bring justice and righteousness to the world, even though it may not happen in the way or timeframe that Habakkuk expects.
*   Habakkuk expresses his trust in God's sovereignty and promises to wait patiently for God's salvation, even in the midst of difficult circumstances.

Key themes:
*   Faith: Habakkuk questions God's justice and righteousness, but ultimately trusts that God knows what he is doing and that he will ultimately bring about justice and righteousness in the world.
*   Justice: Through a dialogue with God, Habakkuk learns that God will ultimately bring justice to the world, even if it is not in the way or the timing that Habakkuk expects.
*   Sovereignty: Habakkuk acknowledges that God is in control of history and that he will accomplish his purposes in his own way and in his own time.
*   Judgment: Habakkuk prophesies the judgment of God against Babylon, as well as against Israel for its sins. Habakkuk recognizes that God's judgment is necessary for justice to be done in the world.
*   Humility: Habakkuk recognizes that he does not have all the answers and that he needs to trust in God, even when he doesn't understand what God is doing. Habakkuk's humility before God allows him to have a deeper faith and trust in God.

Key verse(s):

"But the LORD is in his holy temple: let all the earth keep silence before him." Habakkuk 2:20 KJV

ZEPHANIAH

Overview:
This book contains a series of prophetic messages from the prophet Zephaniah, who speaks out against the idolatry and complacency of the people of Judah. Zephaniah warns that God will judge the people for their sins, but also holds out the possibility of repentance and restoration.

Presumed Author:
Zephaniah

Estimated date written:
650 B.C.

Key events:
- Zephaniah was a prophet who lived during the reign of King Josiah of Judah.
- Zephaniah prophesies against Judah and its surrounding nations, warning them of the coming day of the Lord, a day of judgment and wrath.
- Zephaniah calls for repentance and warns that the Lord will punish those who continue to rebel against him.
- Zephaniah also prophesies about the restoration of Judah and the coming of a righteous king who will bring peace and prosperity to the land.
- Zephaniah ends his book with a song of praise, celebrating God's salvation and restoration of his people.

Key themes:
- Judgment: Zephaniah warns that the day of the Lord is coming, a day of wrath and judgment upon all those who rebel against God.
- Repentance: Zephaniah calls for repentance from the people of Judah, urging them to turn back to God and to seek his mercy and forgiveness.
- Restoration: Zephaniah also prophesies about the restoration of Judah and the coming of a righteous king who will bring peace and prosperity to the land.
- Salvation: Zephaniah ends his book with a song of praise, celebrating God's salvation and restoration of his people.

Key verse(s):

"The LORD thy God in the midst of thee is mighty; he will save, he will rejoice over thee with joy; he will rest in his love, he will joy over thee with singing." Zephaniah 3:17 KJV

HAGGAI

Overview:

This book contains a series of prophetic messages from the prophet Haggai, who encourages the people of Judah to rebuild the Temple that had been destroyed during the Babylonian exile. Haggai promises that if they obey God's command and rebuild the Temple, God will bless them and restore their fortunes.

Presumed Author:

Haggai

Estimated date written:

520 B.C.

Key events:

- Haggai was a prophet who lived during the time of the Persian Empire, after the Jews had returned from exile in Babylon.
- Haggai was sent by God to encourage the Jews who had returned to Jerusalem to rebuild the temple, which had been destroyed by the Babylonians.
- Haggai calls on the people to put aside their own concerns and prioritize the rebuilding of the temple. He reminds them of the importance of having a central place to worship God and of honoring him through their actions.
- The people respond to Haggai's message and begin rebuilding the temple, despite opposition from neighboring nations.
- Haggai delivers a series of messages from God, assuring the people that he will be with them and will bless them for their obedience in rebuilding the temple.

Key themes:

- Rebuilding: The primary theme of the book of Haggai is rebuilding. Haggai encourages the people to rebuild the temple, which had been destroyed years earlier. He emphasizes the importance of having a central place of worship and of honoring God through their actions.
- Obedience: Haggai emphasizes the importance of obedience to God. He urges the people to put aside their own concerns and priorities and to focus on what God has called them to do.
- Blessing: Haggai assures the people that if they obey God and rebuild the temple, He will bless them.
- God's Presence: Haggai reminds the people that the temple is not just a physical building, but a place where God's presence dwells.

Key verse(s):

> "The glory of this latter house shall be greater than of the former, saith the LORD of hosts: and in this place will I give peace, saith the LORD of hosts." Haggai 2:9 KJV

ZECHARIAH

Overview:
This book contains a series of prophetic visions and messages from the prophet Zechariah, who encourages the people of Judah to finish rebuilding the Temple and to live in obedience to God. Zechariah also prophesies about a future Messiah who will come to save Israel and establish His kingdom on earth.

Presumed Author:
> Zechariah

Estimated date written:
> 500 B.C.

Key events:
- Zechariah was a prophet who lived during the time of the Persian Empire, after the Jews had returned from exile in Babylon.
- Like Haggai, Zechariah encouraged the Jews who had returned to Jerusalem to rebuild the temple.
- Zechariah had a series of visions and prophetic messages from God, which he delivered to the people.
- Zechariah's messages included prophecies about the coming of the Messiah, the restoration of Jerusalem, and the future of Israel.
- The book of Zechariah also includes historical accounts of events that took place during Zechariah's time, including the rebuilding of the temple and the crowning of Joshua the high priest.

Key themes:
- Restoration: The primary theme of the book of Zechariah is restoration. Zechariah encourages the people to restore the temple and the city of Jerusalem. He also prophesies about the future restoration of Israel and the coming of the Messiah.
- Repentance: Zechariah emphasizes the importance of repentance. He calls on the people to turn away from their sins and to return to God. He reminds them that their disobedience was the reason they were sent into exile, and that their obedience will bring blessings.
- Messianic Prophecy: Zechariah prophesies about the coming of the Messiah. He describes him as a humble king riding on a donkey, who will bring salvation to the people. He also prophesies about the Messiah's suffering and his eventual victory over evil.
- God's Sovereignty: Zechariah emphasizes the sovereignty of God. He assures the people that God is in control of all things, and that he will fulfill his promises to them.

Key verse(s):

"Then he answered and spake unto me, saying, This is the word of the LORD unto Zerubbabel, saying, Not by might, nor by power, but by my spirit, saith the LORD of hosts."
Zechariah 4:6 KJV

MALACHI

Overview:
This book contains a series of prophetic messages from the prophet Malachi, who speaks out against the religious and moral corruption that were prevalent in Israel during his time. Malachi warns that God will judge the people for their sins, but also holds out the possibility of repentance and restoration. The book ends with a call to remember the law of Moses and to look forward to the coming of the Messiah.

Presumed Author:
> Malachi

Estimated date written:
> 430 B.C.

Key events:
- Malachi was a prophet who lived after the Jews had returned from exile in Babylon.
- The people had become complacent and were not following God's laws, and Malachi rebuked them for their disobedience.
- Malachi's message focused on issues such as neglect of the temple, insincere worship, and unfaithfulness in marriage.
- Malachi also prophesied about the coming of the Messiah and the Day of the Lord, a time of judgment and redemption.

Key themes:
- Covenant: The primary theme of Malachi's message is the covenant between God and his people. Malachi reminds the people of the promises God had made to them, and he calls them to honor their part of the covenant by obeying God's laws and offering sincere worship.
- Repentance: Malachi calls on the people to repent and turn back to God.
- The Messiah: Malachi prophesies about the coming of the Messiah, whom he describes as a refining fire and a purifier, who will bring justice and righteousness to the earth.
- Judgment and Redemption: Malachi prophesies about the Day of the Lord, a time of judgment and redemption. He warns that those who do not repent will face judgment, but those who do will be blessed with the restoration of the temple, the coming of the Messiah, and a time of peace and prosperity.

Key verse(s):

"Bring ye all the tithes into the storehouse, that there may be meat in mine house, and prove me now herewith, saith the LORD of hosts, if I will not open you the windows of heaven, and pour you out a blessing, that there shall not be room enough to receive it." Malachi 3:10 KJV

NEW TESTAMENT

MATTHEW

Overview:
This book is the first of the four Gospels and focuses on the life, teachings, death, and resurrection of Jesus Christ. It emphasizes Jesus' role as the Messiah, or Savior, who fulfills Old Testament prophecies and establishes a new covenant between God and humanity.

Presumed Author:
> Matthew

Estimated date written:
> 55 A.D.

Key events:
- Matthew is the first of the four Gospels in the New Testament and focuses on the life and teachings of Jesus Christ.
- The book begins with Jesus' genealogy and birth, and then follows his ministry, miracles, teachings, and eventual crucifixion and resurrection.
- Some of the key events in Matthew include the Sermon on the Mount (chapters 5-7), the feeding of the 5,000 (chapter 14), Peter's confession of Jesus as the Messiah (chapter 16), and Jesus' triumphal entry into Jerusalem (chapter 21).

Key themes:
- Jesus as the Messiah: Matthew presents Jesus as the long-awaited Messiah, the fulfillment of Old Testament prophecy. He highlights Jesus' genealogy, his birth in Bethlehem, and his miracles and teachings as evidence of his divine identity.
- Jesus is Lord: Jesus is proclaimed as Lord (22:44) within a Godhead (28:19) whose name Emmanuel means "God with us" (1:23) and is worshipped by His followers (14:33, 15:25, 18:26).
- Kingdom of Heaven: Jesus' teachings focus on how to enter and live in this kingdom, which includes leaving behind one's old life and putting Christ above all else.
- Law and Grace: Matthew explores the relationship between the Old Testament law and the New Testament gospel of grace. He shows how Jesus fulfills the law and offers salvation based on faith in Him rather than obedience to the law.

Key verse(s):

"Ask, and it shall be given you; seek, and ye shall find; knock, and it shall be opened unto you:" Matthew 7:7 KJV

MARK

Overview:
This book is the second of the four Gospels and is a concise account of Jesus' ministry and teachings. It emphasizes Jesus' power and authority, as well as His suffering and death on the cross.

Presumed Author:
> Mark

Estimated date written:
> 50 A.D.

Key events:
- Mark is the second of the four Gospels in the New Testament and focuses on the life and ministry of Jesus Christ.
- The book begins with the ministry of John the Baptist and the baptism of Jesus, and then follows Jesus' ministry, miracles, teachings, and eventual crucifixion and resurrection.
- Some of the key events in Mark include the calling of the disciples (chapter 1), the healing of the paralytic (chapter 2), the feeding of the 5,000 (chapter 6), Jesus' transfiguration (chapter 9), and his betrayal and crucifixion (chapters 14-15).

Key themes:
- Jesus as the Son of God: Mark emphasizes Jesus' divinity as the Son of God (1:34), showing how his teachings, miracles, and actions demonstrate his divine authority and power.
- The kingdom of God: Mark highlights the concept of the "kingdom of God," which refers to God's rule and reign on earth. He shows how Jesus' teachings and miracles demonstrate the presence and power of God's kingdom, and how believers are called to participate in building the kingdom through their lives and witness.
- Discipleship: Mark emphasizes the importance of following Jesus as a disciple, showing how Jesus called his disciples to follow him and how they responded. He also shows the challenges and sacrifices involved in discipleship, and the importance of persevering through difficult times.
- The suffering servant: Mark portrays Jesus as the suffering servant who came to give his life as a ransom for many. He emphasizes Jesus' sacrificial death on the cross and shows how it was necessary for the forgiveness of sins and the salvation of humanity.
- The power of faith: Mark highlights the importance of faith in Jesus, showing how it is essential for salvation. He also shows how faith is demonstrated through acts of obedience and service to others.

Key verse(s):

"For what shall it profit a man, if he shall gain the whole world, and lose his own soul?" Mark 8:36 KJV

LUKE

Overview:
This book is the third of the four Gospels and is a detailed and well-researched account of Jesus' life and ministry. It emphasizes Jesus' compassion for the poor and marginalized, as well as His message of salvation for all people.

Presumed Author:
> Luke

Estimated date written:
> 60 A.D.

Key events:
- Luke is the third of the four Gospels in the New Testament and focuses on the life and teachings of Jesus Christ.
- The book begins with the birth of John the Baptist and Jesus' birth, and then follows Jesus' ministry, miracles, teachings, and eventual crucifixion and resurrection.
- Some of the key events in Luke include the parable of the Good Samaritan (chapter 10), the Prodigal Son (chapter 15), the Last Supper (chapter 22), and Jesus' appearance to the disciples after his resurrection (chapter 24).

Key themes:
- Jesus as the Savior: Luke presents Jesus as the Savior of the world (2:11), who came to seek and save the lost. He highlights Jesus' compassion for the poor, sick, and marginalized, and shows how he offers salvation to all who come to him in faith.
- Holy Spirit/Ghost: Luke emphasizes the role of the Holy Spirit (Luke 12:12) in Jesus' life and ministry, as well as in the lives of his followers. He shows how the Holy Spirit empowers believers to share the gospel and live out their faith.
- Women and social outcasts: Luke gives special attention to the role of women and social outcasts in Jesus' ministry. He shows how Jesus welcomed and ministered to people of all backgrounds, including women, the poor, and the disabled (7:36–50).
- Prayer: Luke highlights the importance of prayer in the life of Jesus and his followers. He records several instances where Jesus prays, and shows how prayer was an essential part of the early church's life and ministry.

Key verse(s):

"And he said, The things which are impossible with men are possible with God." Luke 18:27
KJV

JOHN

Overview:
This book is the fourth of the four Gospels and is a theological reflection on the life, teachings, death, and resurrection of Jesus Christ. It emphasizes Jesus' divinity and His role as Lord and Son of God who offers eternal life to those who believe and follow Him.

Presumed Author:
>   John

Estimated date written:
>   90 A.D.

Key events:
- The book of John is the fourth and final Gospel in the New Testament and focuses on the life and teachings of Jesus Christ.
- The book begins by establishing Jesus as the "Word" (v14) and the "Word was God" (v1). It says Jesus existed in the beginning and created everything (v3). It follows his ministry, miracles, teachings, and eventual crucifixion and resurrection.
- Some of the key events in John include the wedding at Cana where Jesus turns water into wine (chapter 2), His encounter with Nicodemus where He teaches about being born again (chapter 3), His interaction with the woman at the well (chapter 4), the healing of the man born blind (chapter 9), and His resurrection appearance to his disciples (chapter 20).

Key themes:
- Eternal life: The book shows how Jesus came to Earth to offer eternal life to those who believe in Him.
- Faith: John emphasizes the importance of faith in Jesus, showing how it is essential for receiving salvation. He also shows how faith is demonstrated through acts of obedience and service to others.
- The Holy Spirit: John highlights the role of the Holy Spirit in the life of believers, showing how the Spirit empowers and guides them in their relationship with God and their service to others. (7:39)
- Love: John emphasizes the importance of love in the Christian life, showing how love for God and for others is the hallmark of a true disciple of Jesus. He also shows how Jesus' love for humanity was demonstrated through his sacrificial death on the cross. (15:10)

Key verse(s):

"For God so loved the world, that he gave his only begotten Son, that whosoever believeth in him should not perish, but have everlasting life." John 3:16 KJV

ACTS

Overview:
This book is a history of the early Christian church, focusing on the ministry of the apostles and the spread of the gospel message throughout the Roman Empire. It emphasizes the power of the Holy Spirit and the importance of sharing the good news of Jesus Christ with others.

Presumed Author:
> Luke

Estimated date written:
> 65 A.D.

Key events:
- The ascension of Jesus Christ (Acts 1:9-11)
- The coming of the Holy Spirit at Pentecost (Acts 2:1-4)
- The healing of a crippled beggar by Peter and John (Acts 3:1-10)
- The martyrdom of Stephen (Acts 7:54-60)
- The conversion of Saul (later known as Paul) on the road to Damascus (Acts 9:1-19)
- The Jerusalem Council, which resolved a dispute between Jewish and Gentile believers over circumcision and other issues (Acts 15:1-35)
- Paul's missionary journeys, during which he spread the gospel to various parts of the Roman Empire (Acts 13-28)

Key themes:
- The birth and growth of the early church.
- The work of the Holy Spirit in empowering believers to share their faith and perform miracles.
- The persecution faced by the early Christians, as well as their perseverance in the face of hardship and opposition.
- The importance of repentance, faith, and baptism.
- The leadership of Peter and Paul in the early church and their respective roles in spreading the gospel to Jews and Gentiles.
- The significance of the resurrection of Jesus Christ as the foundation of Christian faith and hope.

Key verse(s):

> "Then Peter said unto them, Repent, and be baptized every one of you in the name of Jesus Christ for the remission of sins, and ye shall receive the gift of the Holy Ghost." Acts 2:38
> KJV

ROMANS

Overview:

This book is a theological treatise on the nature of salvation and the role of faith in the life of the Christian. It emphasizes the universality of sin and the need for salvation through faith in Jesus Christ.

Presumed Author:

Paul

Estimated date written:

50 - 70 A.D.

Key events:

- The book of Romans is an informational letter written by the apostle Paul to the church in Rome.
- Paul writes about the need for a Savior, faith, how ought to live, Israel's future, and being unified with believers.

Key themes:

- The righteousness of God and the need for all people to be justified by faith (Romans 1:16-17; 3:21-26)
- The universality of sin and the need for all people to repent and turn to God (Romans 1:18-3:20)
- The role of the law in revealing sin and pointing people to Christ (Romans 3:20; 7:7-25)
- The centrality of faith in the work of Christ for salvation (Romans 3:21-31; 4:1-25)
- The freedom from sin and death that comes through Christ (Romans 6:1-23)
- The work of the Holy Spirit in the life of believers, including sanctification and assurance of salvation (Romans 8:1-17)
- The place of Israel in God's plan of salvation (Romans 9-11)
- The call for Christians to live in unity and love (Romans 12:1-21)
- The importance of submission to authority and living in a way that honors God (Romans 13:1-7)
- The significance of the gospel message as the power of God for salvation (Romans 1:16-17; 15:14-33)

Key verse(s):

"Bless them which persecute you: bless, and curse not." Romans 12:14 KJV

1 CORINTHIANS

Overview:

This book is a letter from the apostle Paul to the church in Corinth, addressing various problems and controversies that had arisen in the church. It emphasizes the importance of love, unity, and the proper use of spiritual gifts.

Presumed Author:

Paul

Estimated date written:

50 - 70 A.D.

Key events:

- The founding and establishment of the church in Corinth by the apostle Paul (Acts 18:1-17)
- Paul's subsequent letters and visits to the church to address various issues (1 Corinthians 5:9-13; 2 Corinthians 2:1-4; 13:1-4)

Key themes:

- The importance of unity and the danger of division in the church (1 Corinthians 1:10-17; 3:1-23)
- The need for holiness and purity within the church (1 Corinthians 5:1-13; 6:12-20)
- The proper use and understanding of spiritual gifts (1 Corinthians 12:1-14:40)
- The centrality of Christ and the cross in the Christian message (1 Corinthians 1:18-31; 2:1-5)
- The importance of love as the motivation for Christian living (1 Corinthians 13:1-13)
- The resurrection of the dead and its significance for believers (1 Corinthians 15:1-58)
- The role of women in the church and in marriage (1 Corinthians 11:2-16; 14:34-35)
- The call to use Christian freedom in a way that does not cause stumbling or harm to others (1 Corinthians 8:1-13; 10:23-33)
- The responsibility of Christian leaders to be examples of faith and love (1 Corinthians 4:1-21; 9:1-27)
- The need for believers to flee from idolatry and pursue righteousness (1 Corinthians 10:1-22)

Key verse(s):

"And now abideth faith, hope, charity, these three; but the greatest of these is charity." 1 Corinthians 13:13 KJV

2 Corinthians

Overview:
This book is a second letter from Paul to the church in Corinth, expressing his joy and relief that the church has responded positively to his previous letter. It emphasizes the themes of suffering, weakness, and the power of God's grace.

Presumed Author:
Paul

Estimated date written:
50 - 70 A.D.

Key events:
- Paul's second letter to the Corinthian church, written during his third missionary journey (around 55-57 AD).
- Paul defends his apostleship against false teachers who had infiltrated the church.
- Paul encourages the Corinthian believers to continue giving generously to support the needs of the church in Jerusalem.
- Paul describes his own sufferings and hardships for the sake of the gospel.
- Paul warns the Corinthians to avoid immoral behavior and false teachers.

Key themes:
- The sufficiency of God's grace for salvation and for Christian living.
- The importance of Christian unity and reconciliation.
- The role of suffering and weakness in the life of a believer.
- The contrast between the New Covenant and the Old Covenant.
- The importance of giving generously and sacrificially to support the work of the gospel.
- The need for personal holiness and the dangers of false teaching and false teachers.

Key verse(s):

"(For we walk by faith, not by sight:)" 2 Corinthians 5:7 KJV

"And he said unto me, My grace is sufficient for thee..." 2 Corinthians 12:9 KJV

"Therefore if any man be in Christ, he is a new creature: old things are passed away; behold, all things are become new." 2 Corinthians 5:17 KJV

GALATIANS

Overview:

This book is a letter from Paul to the churches in Galatia, addressing the issue of legalism and the need for salvation through faith in Christ alone. It emphasizes the freedom and power that come through the Holy Spirit.

Presumed Author:

> Paul

Estimated date written:

> 50 - 70 A.D.

Key events:

- Paul's letter to churches in Galatia, likely written during his 2nd missionary journey (around 49-50 AD).
- False teachers had infiltrated the churches, promoting a "different gospel" that required adherence to Jewish laws and customs.
- Paul defends his apostleship and the gospel message he had preached to the Galatians.
- Paul argues that salvation is by faith in Christ alone, apart from works of the law.
- Paul appeals to the Galatians to reject the false teaching and to hold fast to the true gospel.

Key themes:

- The importance of justification by faith alone, apart from works of the law.
- The authority and sufficiency of the gospel message.
- The role of the Mosaic law in the life of a Christian.
- The unity of believers in Christ, regardless of their ethnic or cultural backgrounds.
- The fruit of the Holy Spirit as evidence of a genuine faith.
- The danger of legalism and the need to live by faith in Christ.

Key verse(s):

"There is neither Jew nor Greek, there is neither bond nor free, there is neither male nor female: for ye are all one in Christ Jesus." Galatians 3:28 KJV

"But the fruit of the Spirit is love, joy, peace, longsuffering, gentleness, goodness, faith, Meekness, temperance: against such there is no law." Galatians 5:22 KJV

"For ye are all the children of God by faith in Christ Jesus." Galatians 3:26 KJV

EPHESIANS

Overview:
This book is a letter from Paul to the church in Ephesus, emphasizing the spiritual blessings and unity that believers have in Christ. It also addresses practical issues related to Christian living and the need for spiritual warfare.

Presumed Author:
Paul

Estimated date written:
50 - 70 A.D.

Key events:
- Paul's letter to the Ephesian church, likely written during his imprisonment in Rome (around 60-62 AD).
- The letter was intended not just for the Ephesians, but also for other churches in the region.
- Paul writes to encourage and instruct believers in their faith, emphasizing the unity and diversity of the church.

Key themes:
- The spiritual blessings that believers have in Christ, including adoption, redemption, and forgiveness.
- The importance of unity in the church, which is made up of diverse members united in Christ.
- The role of Christ as the head of the church and the source of its unity.
- The power of God's grace in saving sinners and bringing them into relationship with Him.
- The need for believers to live holy lives, bearing fruit that is pleasing to God.
- The spiritual battle that believers face and the armor of God that they can use to stand firm against the enemy.

Key verse(s):

"For by grace are ye saved through faith; and that not of yourselves: it is the gift of God:"
Ephesians 2:8 KJV

"Husbands, love your wives, even as Christ also loved the church, and gave himself for it;"
Ephesians 5:25 KJV

PHILIPPIANS

Overview:
This book is a letter from Paul to the church in Philippi, expressing his love and gratitude for their support and encouragement. It emphasizes the importance of humility, unity, and joy in the Christian life.

Presumed Author:
> Paul

Estimated date written:
> 50 - 70 A.D.

Key events:
- Philippians is a letter from the Apostle Paul to the church in Philippi, a city in Macedonia.
- Paul wrote the letter while he was in prison, probably in Rome, around AD 60-62.
- The letter contains Paul's thanks and encouragement for the Philippian believers, as well as instructions for Christian living and unity.

Key themes:
- Joy: Paul emphasizes the importance of joy in the Christian life, even in the midst of difficult circumstances. He encourages the Philippians to find joy in Christ and to rejoice always.
- Humility: Paul urges the Philippians to imitate Christ's humility and to consider others as more important than themselves.
- Unity: Paul stresses the importance of unity among believers and urges the Philippians to put aside any divisions or conflicts.
- Faith and righteousness: Paul emphasizes the importance of faith in Christ for salvation and the need for believers to pursue righteousness through the power of the Holy Spirit.
- God's provision: Paul highlights God's faithfulness in providing for believers' needs and encourages the Philippians to trust in God's provision.

Key verse(s):

"Be careful for nothing; but in every thing by prayer and supplication with thanksgiving let your requests be made known unto God. And the peace of God, which passeth all understanding, shall keep your hearts and minds through Christ Jesus." Philippians 4:6-7 KJV

COLOSSIANS

Overview:
This book is a letter from Paul to the church in Colossae, emphasizing the preeminence and sufficiency of Christ in all things. It also addresses practical issues related to Christian living and the need to avoid false teachings.

Presumed Author:
> Paul

Estimated date written:
> 50 - 70 A.D.

Key events:
- Paul writes this letter to the church in Colossae while imprisoned in Rome
- Paul sends Tychicus and Onesimus to Colossae with the letter

Key themes:
- The supremacy of Christ: Paul emphasizes the centrality and preeminence of Christ in all things, both in the spiritual realm and in the material world
- The danger of false teachings: Paul warns the Colossians against false teachings that promote legalism and mysticism, and encourages them to remain grounded in the truth of the gospel
- Christian living: Paul provides practical advice on how to live a life that is pleasing to God, including instructions on relationships, work, and prayer
- Unity in Christ: Paul encourages the Colossians to maintain unity as a church, despite their cultural and ethnic differences, and to work together for the sake of the gospel

Key verse(s):

"For by him were all things created, that are in heaven, and that are in earth, visible and invisible, whether they be thrones, or dominions, or principalities, or powers: all things were created by him, and for him:" Colossians 1:16 KJV

1 THESSALONIANS

Overview:
This book is a letter from Paul to the church in Thessalonica, encouraging and exhorting them to live in light of the coming of Christ. It emphasizes the themes of faith, hope, and love.

Presumed Author:

Paul

Estimated date written:

50 - 70 A.D.

Key events:

- Paul and Silas visit Thessalonica and preach the gospel, resulting in many converts (Acts 17:1-9)
- Persecution arises against the new believers, and Paul is forced to leave the city (Acts 17:10-15)
- Paul sends Timothy to check on the Thessalonians and receives a favorable report (1 Thessalonians 3:1-10)
- Paul writes his first letter to the Thessalonians, encouraging and exhorting them in their faith (1 Thessalonians 1:1-5:28)

Key themes:

- Encouragement in the midst of persecution: Paul writes to encourage the Thessalonians in their faith and to reassure them that their suffering is not in vain, but is part of the Christian life (1 Thessalonians 1:6-10, 2:13-16, 3:1-5)
- Sanctification and holiness: Paul emphasizes the importance of living a holy life and growing in sanctification, exhorting the Thessalonians to abstain from sexual immorality and to live in a way that pleases God (1 Thessalonians 4:1-12)
- The second coming of Christ: Paul addresses the Thessalonians' concerns about the return of Christ and the resurrection of the dead, providing them with hope and assurance of their future in Christ (1 Thessalonians 4:13-18, 5:1-11)
- Love and unity within the church: Paul urges the Thessalonians to love one another and to maintain unity within the church, reminding them that they are all part of the body of Christ (1 Thessalonians 4:9-10, 5:12-15)

Key verse(s):

"Pray without ceasing." 1 Thessalonians 5:17 KJV

"For God hath not appointed us to wrath, but to obtain salvation by our Lord Jesus Christ," 1 Thessalonians 5:9 KJV

2 THESSALONIANS

Overview:

This book is a second letter from Paul to the church in Thessalonica, addressing various concerns and correcting some misunderstandings related to the second coming of Christ.

Presumed Author:

> Paul

Estimated date written:

> 50 - 70 A.D.

Key events:

- Paul wrote this letter to the Thessalonians shortly after writing his first letter to them, in order to address some of the concerns and questions they had raised in response to his teaching.
- The letter emphasizes the return of Jesus Christ, and offers comfort to the Thessalonians who were concerned about the fate of their loved ones who had already died before Christ's return.

Key themes:

- Eschatology: This book focuses on the "end times," with an emphasis on the return of Jesus Christ and the events that will precede it.
- Persecution: The Thessalonian believers were experiencing persecution for their faith, and Paul encourages them to remain steadfast in the face of this opposition.
- Church discipline: Paul also addresses issues related to church discipline, including the importance of confronting and dealing with sin in the church.

Key verse(s):

> "Therefore, brethren, stand fast, and hold the traditions which ye have been taught, whether by word, or our epistle." 2 Thessalonians 2:15 KJV

> "And the Lord direct your hearts into the love of God, and into the patient waiting for Christ." 2 Thessalonians 3:5 KJV

1 TIMOTHY

Overview:

This book is a letter from Paul to his young protégé Timothy, providing instructions and encouragement for his ministry in the church. It emphasizes the importance of sound doctrine, godly character, and proper leadership.

Presumed Author:

> Paul

Estimated date written:

> 50 - 70 A.D.

Key events:

- Paul writes to Timothy, a young pastor in Ephesus, giving him instructions on how to lead the church effectively.
- Paul warns Timothy about false teachers who are spreading false doctrines and encourages him to remain faithful to sound doctrine.
- Paul addresses several issues in the church, such as the roles of men and women, qualifications for leaders, and the care of widows.

Key themes:

- Sound Doctrine: Paul emphasizes the importance of sound doctrine and warns against false teachings that may lead the church astray.
- Leadership: Paul provides instructions for church leaders, including the qualifications for overseers and deacons.
- Prayer: Paul encourages the church to pray for all people, including those in authority, and to lead quiet and peaceful lives.
- Conduct: Paul teaches on the proper conduct for men and women in the church, and on the importance of loving others and caring for those in need.

Key verse(s):

"For the love of money is the root of all evil: which while some coveted after, they have erred from the faith, and pierced themselves through with many sorrows." 1 Timothy 6:10 KJV

2 TIMOTHY

Overview:

This book is a second letter from Paul to Timothy, written shortly before his death, and encouraging him to remain faithful to the gospel message. It emphasizes the need for endurance, the importance of Scripture, and the reality of opposition and persecution.

Presumed Author:

Paul

Estimated date written:

50 - 70 A.D.

Key events:

- Paul writes a letter to Timothy, his beloved co-worker and son in the faith, from prison in Rome (2 Timothy 1:8, 16).

- Paul encourages Timothy to continue in his faith and to boldly proclaim the gospel despite persecution and opposition (2 Timothy 1:7-8, 2:1-2).
- Paul reminds Timothy of the importance of sound doctrine and warns him about false teachers who will arise (2 Timothy 1:13-14, 4:3-4).
- Paul urges Timothy to be strong and faithful in his ministry, even in the face of suffering and hardship (2 Timothy 2:3-7, 4:5).

Key themes:
- Perseverance in faith and ministry despite opposition and suffering (2 Timothy 1:7-8, 2:3-7, 4:5).
- Sound doctrine and the importance of teaching and holding to the truth of the gospel (2 Timothy 1:13-14, 2:15, 3:16-17).
- Warning against false teachers and the need to avoid their influence (2 Timothy 2:16-18, 3:1-9, 4:3-4).
- The ultimate reward of faithful service to Christ (2 Timothy 2:11-13, 4:7-8).

Key verse(s):

"For God hath not given us the spirit of fear; but of power, and of love, and of a sound mind."
2 Timothy 1:7 KJV

TITUS

Overview:
This book is a letter from Paul to his coworker Titus, instructing him on how to oversee the churches on the island of Crete. It emphasizes the importance of sound doctrine, godly character, and good works.

Presumed Author:
Paul

Estimated date written:
50 - 70 A.D.

Key events:
- Paul sent Titus to Crete to set things in order and appoint elders (1:5).
- Paul advised Titus on the qualifications of church leaders (1:6-9).
- Titus was instructed to teach sound doctrine and promote godly living (2:1-10).
- Paul reminded Titus of the gospel's power to save and transform (3:3-7).

Key themes:
- Church leadership: The book of Titus emphasizes the importance of having qualified and godly leaders in the church who can teach sound doctrine and model godly living.

- Good works: Paul stresses the importance of living a godly life and doing good works as a response to God's grace and to reflect the gospel's power to transform lives.
- Salvation by grace: The book of Titus emphasizes the gospel's message that salvation comes through faith in Christ, not through good works or human effort.
- False teaching: Paul warns Titus to beware of false teachers who promote legalism or antinomianism, and to hold fast to the gospel's message of grace.

Key verse(s):

"For the grace of God that bringeth salvation hath appeared to all men," Titus 2:11 KJV

"Not by works of righteousness which we have done, but according to his mercy he saved us, by the washing of regeneration, and renewing of the Holy Ghost;" Titus 3:5 KJV

PHILEMON

Overview:
This book is a personal letter from Paul to his friend Philemon, urging him to forgive his runaway slave Onesimus and receive him back as a brother in Christ. It emphasizes the themes of reconciliation and love.

Presumed Author:
Paul

Estimated date written:
50 - 70 A.D.

Key events:
- Paul writes to Philemon, a wealthy Christian in Colossae, on behalf of Onesimus, a slave who had run away from Philemon and had become a Christian while with Paul.
- Paul appeals to Philemon to forgive Onesimus and welcome him back as a brother in Christ.
- Paul offers to pay any debt owed by Onesimus to Philemon.

Key themes:
- Forgiveness: Paul emphasizes the importance of forgiveness and reconciliation in the Christian community. He urges Philemon to forgive Onesimus and treat him as a brother in Christ.
- Equality: Paul emphasizes the equal status of all believers in Christ, regardless of social class or background. He calls Onesimus Philemon's "son" and "brother" in Christ, rather than referring to him as a slave.

- Love: Paul demonstrates his own love for Philemon and Onesimus, and encourages them to love one another as members of the Christian community.
- Responsibility: Paul reminds Philemon of his responsibility to care for and protect his slaves, while at the same time appealing to him to treat Onesimus with compassion and forgiveness.

Key verse(s):

"That the communication of thy faith may become effectual by the acknowledging of every good thing which is in you in Christ Jesus." Philemon 1:6 KJV

HEBREWS

Overview:
This book is a sermon or letter that emphasizes the superiority of Jesus Christ and the new covenant over the old covenant. It emphasizes the themes of faith, perseverance, and the superiority of Christ's sacrifice.

Presumed Author:
> Unknown

Estimated date written:
> 65 A.D.

Key events:
- The author of Hebrews exhorts his audience to hold fast to their faith in Jesus Christ and warns them against the dangers of falling away (Hebrews 2:1-4; 3:7-4:13; 10:19-39).
- The author also provides a detailed comparison between the Old Covenant, based on the law of Moses, and the New Covenant, based on the sacrifice of Jesus Christ (Hebrews 8:1-13; 9:1-28).
- The author emphasizes the supremacy of Jesus Christ as the great high priest who offers a once-for-all sacrifice for sins, and encourages his readers to approach God with confidence through Jesus (Hebrews 4:14-16; 7:1-28; 10:1-18).

Key themes:
- The superiority of Jesus Christ over all other religious figures and systems, including angels, Moses, and the Levitical priesthood.
- The danger of apostasy and the importance of holding fast to faith in Jesus Christ.
- The fulfillment of Old Testament prophecies and the superiority of the New Covenant based on the sacrifice of Jesus Christ.
- The need for perseverance and endurance in the face of trials and suffering, and the encouragement of a community of believers.
- The power of faith in Jesus Christ to transform lives and provide access to the presence of God.

Key verse(s):

"Now faith is the substance of things hoped for, the evidence of things not seen." Hebrews 11:1 KJV

JAMES

Overview:

This book is a letter from James, likely the brother of Jesus, addressing practical issues related to Christian living and the need to put faith into action. It emphasizes the importance of good works, perseverance, and controlling one's tongue.

Presumed Author:

James

Estimated date written:

45 A.D.

Key events:

- The book of James does not recount any specific events, but it is believed to have been written by James, the brother of Jesus, to a Jewish Christian audience.

Key themes:

- Faith and Works: James emphasizes the importance of not only having faith, but also putting that faith into action through good works. He argues that true faith will naturally result in good works, and that without works, faith is dead.
- Wisdom and Speech: James warns against the dangers of unwise and hurtful speech, and encourages his readers to seek wisdom from God and use their speech to build others up rather than tear them down.
- Trials and Perseverance: James acknowledges the reality of trials and suffering in the Christian life, but encourages his readers to persevere and remain steadfast in their faith, trusting that God is ultimately in control.
- Social Justice: James advocates for caring for the poor and marginalized, and denounces favoritism and discrimination within the church community. He stresses the importance of showing mercy and doing good to others as evidence of true faith.

Key verse(s):

"Humble yourselves in the sight of the Lord, and he shall lift you up." James 4:10 KJV

"But be ye doers of the word, and not hearers only, deceiving your own selves." James 1:22 KJV

1 PETER

Overview:
This book is a letter from Peter to the churches in Asia Minor, encouraging believers to endure persecution and live as witnesses for Christ. It emphasizes the themes of suffering, hope, and the example of Christ's suffering.

Presumed Author:
Peter

Estimated date written:
60 A.D.

Key events:
- Written by Peter, one of the twelve apostles of Jesus Christ.
- Written between AD 60 and 65, most likely from Rome during Peter's imprisonment under Emperor Nero.
- Addresses Christians who were undergoing persecution and suffering for their faith.

Key themes:
- The hope and salvation that Christians have through faith in Jesus Christ.
- The importance of living a holy and righteous life in the face of persecution and suffering.
- The concept of being "living stones" built into a spiritual house, with Christ as the cornerstone.
- The idea of submitting to earthly authorities while remaining loyal to God.
- The example of Christ's suffering and death as a model for enduring persecution and suffering.
- The call to love one another and serve one another in humility.

Key verse(s):
- "Blessed be the God and Father of our Lord Jesus Christ! By his great mercy he has given us a new birth into a living hope through the resurrection of Jesus Christ from the dead" (1 Peter 1:3).
- "Beloved, do not be surprised at the fiery ordeal that is taking place among you to test you, as though something strange were happening to you. But rejoice insofar as you are sharing Christ's sufferings, so that you may also be glad and shout for joy when his glory is revealed" (1 Peter 4:12-13).
- "Like newborn infants, long for the pure, spiritual milk, so that by it you may grow into salvation— if indeed you have tasted that the Lord is good" (1 Peter 2:2-3).
- "For it is better to suffer for doing good, if suffering should be God's will, than to suffer for doing evil" (1 Peter 3:17).
- "Above all, maintain constant love for one another, for love covers a multitude of sins" (1 Peter 4:8).

"Be sober, be vigilant; because your adversary the devil, as a roaring lion, walketh about, seeking whom he may devour:" 1 Peter 5:8 KJV

2 PETER

Overview:
This book is a second letter from Peter, warning against false teachers and encouraging believers to grow in their knowledge of Christ. It emphasizes the themes of knowledge, godliness, and the importance of Scripture.

Presumed Author:
Peter

Estimated date written:
60 A.D.

Key events:
- The author identifies himself as Simon Peter, a servant and apostle of Jesus Christ (2 Peter 1:1).
- The author encourages his readers to grow in their faith and reminds them of the promises of God (2 Peter 1:3-4).
- The author warns against false teachers who will introduce destructive heresies (2 Peter 2:1-3).
- The author affirms the truth of the Scriptures and the reliability of the message preached by the apostles (2 Peter 1:16-21; 3:1-2).
- The author emphasizes the coming judgment of God and encourages his readers to live holy and godly lives (2 Peter 3:7-13).

Key themes:
- The importance of growth in the Christian faith (2 Peter 1:5-8).
- The reality of false teachers and the need to be discerning in what we believe (2 Peter 2:1-3; 3:17-18).
- The reliability and authority of the Scriptures (2 Peter 1:16-21).
- The reality of the coming judgment of God (2 Peter 3:7-13).
- The call to live holy and godly lives in light of these truths (2 Peter 3:11-14).

Key verse(s):

"But the day of the Lord will come as a thief in the night; in the which the heavens shall pass away with a great noise, and the elements shall melt with fervent heat, the earth also and the works that are therein shall be burned up." 2 Peter 3:10 KJV

1 JOHN

Overview:
This book is a letter from John, addressing issues related to false teaching and emphasizing the importance of love, obedience, and fellowship with God. It emphasizes the themes of love, light, and truth.

Presumed Author:
John

Estimated date written:
90 A.D.

Key events:
- There are no specific events mentioned in the book of 1 John
- The author, traditionally believed to be the apostle John, writes to a group of Christians to address some of their concerns and to offer them encouragement.

Key themes:
- Love: John emphasizes the importance of love for one another as a hallmark of being a follower of Jesus Christ. He says that anyone who claims to love God but hates their brother or sister is a liar.
- Light and Darkness: John contrasts light and darkness, with light representing God and goodness, and darkness representing sin and evil.
- Sin: John acknowledges that believers are not perfect and will sin, but he also emphasizes the importance of confessing our sins and receiving forgiveness through Jesus Christ.
- Truth: John stresses the importance of knowing and believing in the truth, particularly the truth about Jesus Christ and his teachings. He warns against false teachers who distort the truth and lead people astray.
- Assurance: John wants his readers to have assurance of their salvation and to know that they have eternal life through their faith in Jesus Christ. He encourages them to abide in Christ and to keep his commandments.

Key verse(s):

"There is no fear in love; but perfect love casteth out fear: because fear hath torment. He that feareth is not made perfect in love." 1 John 4:18 KJV

2 JOHN

Overview:

This book is a second letter from John, warning against false teachers and encouraging believers to continue walking in the truth. It emphasizes the importance of love and obedience.

Presumed Author:

John

Estimated date written:

90 A.D.

Key events:

- The author, who identifies himself as "the elder," writes a letter to a chosen lady and her children, warning them against false teachers who deny Jesus Christ's coming in the flesh.
- The elder exhorts the recipients to love one another and to abide in the truth of Christ.

Key themes:

- Truth and love: The elder emphasizes the importance of abiding in the truth of Christ and loving one another as the key to spiritual health and fellowship.
- Hospitality and discernment: The elder instructs the recipients to show hospitality to true teachers who abide in the truth of Christ, while rejecting false teachers who do not.
- Walking in obedience: The elder encourages the recipients to continue walking in obedience to Christ's commandments and to avoid falling into deception.

Key verse(s):

"And this is love, that we walk after his commandments. This is the commandment, That, as ye have heard from the beginning, ye should walk in it." 2 John 1:6 KJV

"Whosoever transgresseth, and abideth not in the doctrine of Christ, hath not God. He that abideth in the doctrine of Christ, he hath both the Father and the Son." 2 John 1:9 KJV

3 John

Overview:
This book is a third letter from John, praising a man named Gaius for his hospitality and support of the gospel message. It also addresses the negative influence of a man named Diotrephes and encourages believers to imitate good examples.

Presumed Author:
John

Estimated date written:
90 A.D.

Key events:
- This book is a personal letter written by John to Gaius, one of his close friends and a leader in a local church.
- John commends Gaius for his faithfulness and support of traveling missionaries, and encourages him to continue his good work.
- John also criticizes a man named Diotrephes, who is causing problems in the church and refuses to accept John's authority as an apostle.
- John plans to visit Gaius and the church soon and hopes to see them in person.

Key themes:
- Hospitality: John commends Gaius for his hospitality towards traveling missionaries and encourages other believers to follow his example.
- Faithfulness: John praises Gaius for his faithfulness to the truth and his commitment to serving God.
- Church leadership: John criticizes Diotrephes for his abusive behavior and refusal to submit to apostolic authority, highlighting the importance of having godly leaders in the church.
- Truth and error: John warns his readers to be discerning and avoid false teachers who spread false teachings.

Key verse(s):

"I have no greater joy than to hear that my children walk in truth." 3 John 1:4 KJV

"Beloved, follow not that which is evil, but that which is good. He that doeth good is of God:
but he that doeth evil hath not seen God." 3 John 1:11 KJV

JUDE

Overview:
This book is a letter from Jude, warning against false teachers and encouraging believers to contend for the faith once delivered to the saints. It emphasizes the themes of faith, warning, and the judgment of false teachers.

Presumed Author:
Jude

Estimated date written:
60 A.D.

Key events:
- The author (Jude) wrote a letter to a group of believers warning them against false teachers who were promoting ungodly behavior.
- These false teachers were denying the authority of Jesus Christ and leading people astray with their false teachings.
- Jude encouraged the believers to stand firm in their faith, to remember the teachings of the apostles, and to pray in the Holy Spirit.

Key themes:
- Contending for the faith: Jude urges his readers to "contend for the faith that was once for all entrusted to the saints" (v. 3). He warns them of false teachers who have crept in among them and are perverting the grace of God into sensuality.
- God's judgment: Jude uses examples from the Old Testament to show that God will judge those who rebel against Him and lead others astray. He reminds his readers that even angels who sinned were cast into hell, and that Sodom and Gomorrah were destroyed as an example to others.
- The importance of sound doctrine: Jude encourages his readers to remember the teachings of the apostles and to build themselves up in their most holy faith. He emphasizes the importance of sound doctrine and warns against those who would distort the truth.

Key verse(s):

"To the only wise God our Saviour, be glory and majesty, dominion and power, both now and ever. Amen." Jude 1:25 KJV

REVELATION

Overview:

This book is a prophetic vision that emphasizes the ultimate victory of God and His kingdom over the forces of evil. It describes the end of the world, the return of Christ, and the final judgment, as well as the new heaven and new earth that God will create. It emphasizes the themes of worship, judgment, and hope in the ultimate triumph of God's plan.

Presumed Author:

John

Estimated date written:

90 A.D.

Key events:

- The revelation of Jesus Christ to John on the island of Patmos (1:9-20)
- The letters to the seven churches of Asia (chapters 2-3)
- The vision of the throne room of God (chapter 4)
- The opening of the seven seals of the scroll, resulting in various judgments on the earth (chapters 5-8)
- The sounding of seven trumpets, leading to more judgments on the earth (chapters 8-11)
- The visions of a woman and a dragon, the beast from the sea, and the mark of the beast (chap. 12-13)
- The vision of the Lamb and the 144,000 on Mount Zion (chapter 14)
- The pouring out of the seven bowls of God's wrath (chapters 15-16)
- The description of Babylon the great, the mother of prostitutes, and her destruction (chapters 17-18)
- The second coming of Christ and the battle of Armageddon (chapter 19)
- The binding of Satan, the thousand-year reign of Christ, and the final judgment (chapter 20)
- The description of the new heaven and new earth, and the New Jerusalem (chapters 21-22)

Key themes:

- The revelation of Jesus Christ as the exalted and glorified Son of God, who reigns over all things
- The reality of suffering and persecution for the followers of Christ, and the hope of future vindication and reward
- The call to repentance, faith, endurance, and perseverance in the face of trials and tribulations

Key verse(s):

"And God shall wipe away all tears from their eyes; and there shall be no more death, neither sorrow, nor crying, neither shall there be any more pain: for the former things are passed away." Revelation 21:4 KJV

Publisher Information

By Pure Truth Publications

© Copyright 2023. All rights reserved.

We hope you benefitted from this book or ebook. Please visit other titles through the website or Amazon store. Proceeds help spread Christian publications online.

Browse other Christian ebooks on our website. It includes dozens of **free downloads**:

https://puretruthpublications.com/

Amazon store:

https://www.amazon.com/stores/Pure-Truth-Publications/author/B07N2Q7D6T

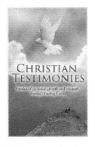

Christian Testimonies: Stories of personal growth and triumph through finding God

★★★★★ 12

Kindle Edition

$2⁹⁹ kindleunlimited

Other formats: Paperback

Inspirational Bible Verses & Pictures: Most popular Bible verse quotes for prayer and...

★★★★★ 26

Kindle Edition

$2⁹⁹ $15.98

Other formats: Paperback

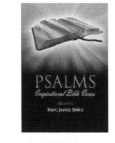

Psalms Inspirational Bible Verses: From the King James Bible

★★★★★ 1

Kindle Edition

$5⁹⁹ $12.58

Other formats: Paperback

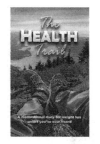

The Health Trail: A motivational story for weight loss unlike you've ever heard

★★★★★ 2

Kindle Edition

$0⁹⁹ $9.58

Other formats: Paperback

Made in the USA
Middletown, DE
06 May 2024

53926047R00042